The Year of YOU: A 10 Step Plan for Reinventing Your Life

KASSANDRA VAUGHN

CONTENTS

YOUR THREE FREE GIFTS

I so appreciate that you invested in the purchase of this book and that you're taking the time to read it. In the spirit of gratitude, I'd like to offer you three free gifts that are exclusive to my book and blog readers (you won't find this offer anywhere else).

The first free gift is a powerful resourced called **7 Simple Ways to Be More Consistent**. If you're looking for a quick, effective guide to developing your focus and consistency muscles, this is it!

To grab your copy of **7 Simple Ways to Be More Consistent**, click here or go to https://kassandravaughn.lpages.co/consistency7ways/.

Your next gift is a **reinvention plan** template that we'll go over in this book. If you're looking for a step-by-step blueprint to help you reinvent your life, click below and **download the reinvention plan template.** that will help you overcome that.

>>>Tap HERE to download your reinvention plan template<<<
https://kassandravaughn.lpages.co/yourreinventionplan/

Your third gift is a daily dose of inspiration that will be sent to your inbox every day! I love to share my life journey with my tribe: the ups, the downs and, of course, the life lessons. If you're ready for a daily email that's going to give you inspiration, transformation and a get-it-together-talk every single day, this is the daily dose for you! Click below and start getting the emails tomorrow!

>>>Tap HERE to sign up for the daily dose<<<
https://kassandravaughn.lpages.co/dailydoseofinspiration/

INTRODUCTION

Your new life is going to cost you your old one.
- Unknown

What could your life look like if you gave yourself FULL permission to completely reinvent it? I'm not talking about a tweak here and a tweak there. What if you gave up all the notions of limitation and lack and reconstructed your entire life in EXACTLY the way you want it to be?

What would that life look like?
What would you look like?
Who would you be?
Where would you go?
Where would you live?
What would every day of your life now feel like?

Far too many are afraid to ask the above questions. They're afraid to hope or dream of a completely different life… or maybe they have and have made some attempt to reinvent themselves… only to return back to who they've always been.

If that's you and you're afraid to go for reinvention again, you're reading the right book. I'm going to help you overcome that fear and move forward with creating your best life. If you've never tried to reinvent yourself, this is also the right book for you. I'm going to give you the steps of reinvention and we're going to walk through the journey to doing it together.

I used to think that reinvention was all about the external. When I was in my twenties and going through secondary infertility, I got so tired of not getting pregnant that I finally gave up the quest to have another baby and, instead, focused completely on reinventing myself. I changed careers and went from being a professor to a personal trainer. I learned about the body and, as I trained other women, I lost sixty pounds. I worked out 2 hours a day, six days a week, and gave up caffeine, sugar, and dairy. By the end of a year of that, I was in the best shape of my life feeling absolutely amazing!

3

And then I got pregnant naturally two months later. My year or so of reinvention was miraculous on all levels.

Now… over the course of that high-risk pregnancy, I gained those sixty pounds back, delivered a preemie 5 pound baby, and was, once again, introduced to the land of reinvention. I was not the fit, personal trainer I had been a year before so one of my biggest lessons (and I'm still learning this one) is that reinvention is so much more about the internal than it is about the external. In fact, I've learned over time that if you want your reinvention to last, the piece to focus on is not what's happening on the outside but what's transforming on the inside.

Over the course of this book, I'm going to talk about each of the following:
- ✓ What reinvention requires of you
- ✓ The steps of reinvention
- ✓ How to reinvent yourself in a way that lasts
- ✓ How to do reinvention when you don't have support
- ✓ How to stay the course on reinvention
- ✓ How to believe in yourself when no one else does

And I'm writing that book from a firm belief that you can be who you want to be. There are no limits. I have recreated myself more times than I can count. I am a coach, a speaker, a mentor, an author, a former personal trainer, a podcaster, and an entrepreneur who loves to speak, teach and learn. At some point in the future, I will become an IFBB Bikini Pro and, amidst all of those different versions of me, here's what I know to be true: you CAN reinvent your life at any point, at any age, at any stage, no matter what the current temporary circumstances might be.

There was a time when I thought I'd be a woman who could only bear one child. Now I have three and hope for more. There was a time when I was a pregnant teenager who everybody said would be a college dropout. Not only did I graduate college ON TIME at 20 but I went on to get my MBA, a master's in Instructional Design, and I'm now working towards a law degree AND I was a professor at the age of 22.

No one can tell you the limits to your ability to reinvent yourself. Only you can decide that.

So let's move forward with open minds and open hearts because THIS is the journey of a lifetime and it's completely in your hands...

Thank you for purchasing **The Year of You: A 10 Step Plan for Reinventing Your Life.**

Kassandra

CHAPTER 1: WHAT DOES IT MEAN TO REINVENT YOURSELF?

Don't ever feel like your best days are behind you.
Reinvention is the purest form of hope. Make today your best yet.
- Phil Wohl

My definition of reinvention has changed over the years. When I was 14 doubling up on Honors and AP classes in the hopes of going to college at 16, I saw college as the most amazing, biggest form of reinvention I could think of at that time. So it's no surprise that when I got to college, I had all of these expectations about how 'different' life was going to be... only I was still me and life was still life... and I didn't understand the difference between external and internal reinvention.

For example, I got to college with a used 1987 Ford Escort and an entirely new wardrobe. I changed my clothes at least three times a day (in between classes) and drove my newfound college friends around at night. I felt like a rock star because of the external things I had going for me. But I wasn't doing any internal work.

I attended a liberal arts college in upstate New York that has one of the most beautiful college campuses in the world. There's a Steinway piano in every dorm. Students get their own room by sophomore year and can live in one of the off-campus apartments by junior year. I went to college lavishing in the decadence and feeling like I could do anything. I wanted to take piano lessons and I thought "Wow! I'm finally going to get to do that here." I wanted to work out more in the amazing gym on campus and I thought, "Wow! I'm finally going to get to do that here." I wanted to go all in on pre-med and thought, "Wow! Their pre-meds get into medical school and do well in life."

But I never sat back and asked myself, at 16 years old, "What's the cost? How much do I have to put in to fully utilize what's here? How many hours a day will that require of me and do I really have the time to do those things?" I never counted the cost and quickly started to feel overwhelmed by all of it. When I went to the music hall to learn about taking piano lessons, I discovered that even intro piano lessons are by audition and acceptance only. I'd never played piano in my life so there went that idea. When I found myself needing to study long hours and focus on learning science concepts that never came to me naturally, I found no time to go to the gym and when I did go to the gym, it was intermittent at best. I spent way too much time partying on the weekends and paying for it during the week and, before long, I realized I wasn't devoting enough time to being pre-med. Eventually, I came to the conclusion that pre-med wasn't what I wanted. I was still living my mother's dream and not pursuing my own.

Why am I telling you all of this?

Because I didn't count the cost at 16. I don't know that I was mature enough to do that back then. I had all of these plans for reinvention and all of these ideas about what I'd do as soon as I 'left home' only to realize that no matter where I went, I was still bringing me with me. It was ME that had to shift first, not the environment, not the circumstances, and certainly not other people.

That lesson has permeated my entire life. When Jon Kabat Zin says "Wherever you go, there you are", he wasn't kidding. We bring ourselves with us wherever we go so reinvention is not necessarily about changing our environment so much as it's about changing how we show up in it.

And college was the first lesson for me in the truth of where reinvention really starts.

What is reinvention?

The Merriam Webster definition of reinvention goes something like this:
> ➢ *To make as if for the first time something already invented*
> ➢ *To remake or redo completely*
> ➢ *To bring into use again*

From this definition, it's clear that reinvention is about taking something that already exists and remaking it completely. However, the kind of reinvention we're talking about needs to be defined on an entirely different level.

Here's my definition of reinvention in the Year of YOU:

Reinvention is the conscious, soul-driven, strategic creation of the highest version of yourself through the destruction of old ways of being, the creation of an entirely different life and the fulfillment of your life's calling in a way that is filled with love, appreciation and joy for self and others.

There's a lot in that definition so let's talk about what this definition of reinvention requires.

Reinvention requires:
- ➢ Coming from the soul
- ➢ Having a strategic focus and understanding of what you want your life to look like
- ➢ Having faith that you can and will become the highest version of yourself
- ➢ A willingness to be both a Creator and a Destroyer
- ➢ Trusting your life's calling and going with that, even in the face of disapproval from others or current, temporary setbacks
- ➢ Knowing that the best way you can be in relationship with others comes by first honoring the calling and relationship you have with yourself

Coming from the soul
Coming from the soul requires that you know how to listen to your own soul. You are a wise being that has lived MANY lifetimes. Each time, you've come into this world with new lessons to learn, new opportunities to take hold of and a new life to go on an adventure with. So many people are living shallow lives where they spend no time getting quiet, still and listening to their own souls. No wonder they have no clue which direction to take their lives in!

Coming from the soul requires that you listen to your intuition on a daily basis. Meditate for 20 to 30 minutes a day (50 minutes is even better). Do practices such as yoga, deep breathing and soul journeys as a way to get closer to hearing the wisdom within. Ancient civilizations practiced this on a daily basis. In many cultures, this is still practiced. Do not allow the speed of life to keep you from hearing your own soul. Without the wisdom within, you'll make a lot of poor life decisions that will cost you time, energy, and focus. The best reinventions come when they originate from the soul.

Having a strategic focus
Lasting reinvention requires that you get crystal clear on the life you want to create. That means knowing exactly what that life looks like, feels like, and why it's a NON-NEGOTIABLE that you get there. You've got to be so sold on the life you're creating that nothing and no one can keep you from it. Even when you have no clue HOW you're going to get there, when you have a strategic focus, you are so clear on the existence of that life that you run in its direction and figure out the hows along the way.

Having faith in yourself and the process of life
In order to reinvent yourself, you have to have faith that even if you don't know how to do it, something inside of you does. It's a mustard seed of faith but it goes a long, long way. There also has to be faith in the process of life. Do some soul searching. Is life FOR you… or AGAINST you? The truth of the answer to that question will let you know what to work on so your reinvention can take place and last. Trusting the process of life requires deciding every single day what world you live in.

Albert Einstein put it like this:
The most important decision we make is whether we believe we live in a friendly or hostile universe.

A willingness to be both a Creator and a Destroyer
A new life requires space. There is no space to create a new life where you refuse to release, surrender or destroy remnants of your old life that no longer serve. Reinvention requires dying to the old so you can give birth to

the new and there is no way around this. Far too often, we're afraid to let things go or to destroy things that, deep down, we know needs destroying.

Trusting your life's calling and going with that, even in the face of disapproval from others or temporary, current setbacks
To reinvent your life, you have to trust your life's calling. And here's the thing to remember:

You don't choose your calling. Your calling chooses you.
- Dr. Wayne Dyer

In order to live your calling, you have to trust it. I don't mean 'sorta-kinda-hope-I-trust-it' but complete and total trust that your life is meant to go in a positive direction and that you have everything within you to make that happen. It's especially important to trust your life's calling when those around you don't understand your path. Self-trust is the only way to ensure that you close your ears to the naysayers and continue going your own way.

Knowing that the best way you can be in relationship with others comes by first honoring the calling and relationship you have with yourself
You are your longest relationship. The key to putting your ALL into reinventing your life comes in knowing the truth of that statement. You are responsible for cultivating and enriching the longest relationship you will ever have. Everything springs from your relationship with you. To reinvent your life, you have to know yourself on a deep level. You have to appreciate, respect and love yourself on an even deeper level. All of that requires creating a relationship with yourself that is grounded, strong and maintained.

At the end of the day, reinvention is much more an internal shift than it is an external change. The work you do on the inside produces the results others see on the outside. Once you understand the deep, inner journey that is reinvention, you can now turn to the 10 steps of reinvention that we're going to talk about throughout this book. While we're going to spend the rest of this book going through each of the ten steps, please dedicate a journal to your reinvention journey and jot down the 10 steps below on the first page of your journal.

The 10 Steps of Reinvention:

1. Get over the idea of being selfish
2. Decide WHO you want to be
3. Create the WHY you need to get there
4. Count the cost
5. Forecast the timelines
6. Develop a MAP (Massive Action Plan) and make different decisions
7. Set up an inevitable environment
8. Speak and act differently
9. Keep your commitments to you
10. Believe in yourself when no one else does

CHAPTER 2: GET OVER THE IDEA OF BEING SELFISH

Never feel guilty for doing what's best for you.
- Unknown

In my family, I'm the oldest of two children. My brother and I are three years apart. While I always loved my little brother, I spent the first ten or so years of his life being VERY jealous of even having a little brother. I did all kinds of mean big sister things to him. I'd hit him when my mom wasn't looking. I'd make him play teacher with me and keep him in the classroom doing work well past his I'm-done-with-school crying point. I even pushed him one time and he hit his head on the corner of a wooden coffee table and had to have quite a few stitches. So it goes without saying that there were many times when my mother would say to me "Kassandra! You're so selfish!" In Haitian terms, she'd call me a **vakabon**. I always thought vakabon meant 'selfish' in Creole but having just looked up the definition in a Haitian dictionary, here's what vakabon actually means:

Bad boy, rascal, hoodlum, jokester, punk, troublemaker

And troublemaker I was at times... especially when it came to my little brother.

I got told I was selfish a lot growing up. I think it was my mother's way of trying to teach me generosity and sharing. How I internalized that was quite different. Because I felt so inherently selfish, I spent many years trying to 'prove' that I wasn't selfish. Over the course of decades and relationships, I became a human doormat, people pleasing and focusing so completely on the needs of others that I neglected the care of myself. It was my way of 'making up' for the selfish person I'd grown up thinking I was.

But there's a problem with that. When you sacrifice yourself for others, you don't win their love. You lose their respect. And it took me a long time to learn that lesson… and I'm still learning. Funny enough, when my mother hit her 40s, she was very clear on telling the world "I'm going through a selfish phase." Looking back on it, my mother had played selfless for far too long and, like my mother, when I hit 40, I finally got to the place of being ready to go through my own 'selfish phase.'

And selfish phases are required for reinvention. You will not reinvent your life and sustain that reinvention until and unless you can give yourself permission to be selfish.

What does that mean?

Reinventing yourself is going to take a lot of time, energy and effort. I wish I could tell you that you can do reinvention in 4 hours a week. That's not how it works. Not only will reinvention require a ton of time every single week but it will require persistence and consistency for a very long period of time to both create the reinvention and build the lifestyle and habits necessary to sustain it.

To do that, you have to be focused on YOUR priorities, even at the expense of other people's demands on you. There is no balance in this equation. When you decide to reinvent your life, one of the first things you're going to have to do is look at how you're spending your time and decide what your top priorities are… and then decrease, delay or remove anything in your life that doesn't sync up with those priorities. To a lot of people, that will look like you being selfish.

For example, when you decide that getting fit is a priority so you now spend 1 to 2 hours a day working out and you're unwilling to budge on that workout time for any reason, the people in your life who were used to you bending to their will and jumping when they called will feel like you're selfish for putting your fitness goals before them. When you decide that you're going back to college and you now have to study twenty hours a week so you no longer can babysit your sister's three children whenever she needs a 'break' from them and you tell her 'No', she's going to assume that you are a different person and you're so self-centered that you're no longer there for her in the way that she's accustomed to.

Get used to being called selfish when you make YOU a priority in your life.

Reinvention requires attention. You will not reinvent your life without being willing to devote ample time to the reinvention process. There are no shortcuts to this. It's one of the reasons why people forego reinventing their lives. They're not prepared to deal with the conflict and the backlash that they'll receive from people who are used to them putting others before themselves… and it's necessary if reinvention is what you actually do.

How do you get over the idea of being selfish?

There are effective and ineffective ways of getting over the idea of being selfish. I'll start with the ineffective ways because so many of us do it.

Ineffective Way #1: Hit a breaking point and kick everybody to the curb.

In many situations, we wait until we get so pissed off by how we're being treated by others that we finally get sick and tired of being sick and tired and kick the people-pleasing and putting ourselves last to the curb immediately. This is the pain threshold experience that most people must go through before they finally decide to put themselves first. Whether that's a bitter breakup, a family drama, or a health crisis that forces a person to put their needs first, this kind of do-or-die experience forces the individual to see how little they value themselves and how much they've taught other people how to treat them badly. The anger, frustration, disappointment and utter rage that results produces an emotional volcanic eruption that then leads to the individual cutting out the selfless behavior and immediately focusing on themselves. This is super ineffective but is what most people tend to do. By the time you've hit your breaking point, you've probably spent more years not caring for yourself and you cannot get those years back. And then you cripple your relationships with others as a result of the aftermath of emotionally exploding on everyone. It's a lose-lose approach.

Ineffective Way #2: Baby stepping your way to making yourself a priority.

Taking small steps is important to achieving any goal, including reinvention. However, there are those who, out of fear and a desire to not completely step out of comfort zones, decide that the best way they can get over the idea of being selfish is by being a 'little bit' selfish a little bit of the time. What this winds up looking like is a person who takes baby steps into making themselves a priority but these baby steps are so small that reinvention doesn't happen. In this way, people literally do a tiny bit here and there for years and still aren't any different in their lives than they were when they started. Yes, they feel better. Yes, they are moving in the direction of putting themselves first but no reinvention is occurring. Why? Because reinvention loves speed and this is not a fast approach to take.

Ineffective Way #3: Go into loner mode so there's no confrontation about your selfishness.

The third way that a lot people get over the idea of being selfish comes through becoming a loner, not having to deal with others, and being free (now that there aren't other people you have to take into consideration) to put yourself first. Sometimes, the loner mode is initiated by a break-up. At other times, the loner mode is brought into being by distancing yourself from family and friends. The problem with this strategy is that it's a band aid on a gunshot wound. You're making yourself a priority by not dealing with the relationships and situations that caused you to NOT make yourself a priority. Yes, you're being selfish and you're able to focus on you but you're doing that in a vacuum. Once you reintroduce family and friends back into your life, you're still going to have to deal with the fact that you have the tendency to people please and put yourself last in those situations. Cutting them out for a short period of time gives you a break from having to do the work of setting boundaries, managing conflict and protecting your time. At some point, you're still going to have to do that. Running from the problem or postponing dealing with the problem doesn't save you from having to eventually confront and handle the problem.

Those are three ineffective ways to get over the idea of being selfish. If you're doing any of the above, it's important to face the fact that you're using an ineffective way to make yourself a priority. Once you face that, now it's time to replace the ineffective strategy with a more effective one.

Here are three effective ways to get over the idea of being selfish:

Effective Way #1: Resign as Manager of the Universe.

So much of putting other people before yourself comes from this idea that you are so crucial to other people's lives that if you aren't the one helping them or taking care of them, they'd be absolutely lost in life and would wind up in a bad situation. At first glance, that seems like a very altruistic, giving mindset to come from. But take a step back and really think about what you're saying. When you believe that you are the ONLY person who can meet the needs of someone else, what you're literally saying is that God isn't good enough to help that person figure out their own problems. You're also saying that the person isn't smart enough or resourceful enough to find a way to get their needs met without your help. More than that, you are taking on the role of Manager of the Universe and carrying someone else's weight on your shoulders… and it's not your burden to carry.

One of the best things you can do to get over the idea of being selfish is recognize that you are not the end-all-be-all for any person in your life. They are equipped with the ability to be resourceful, to get their needs met and they aren't limited to just you for help. They can figure out how to make their lives work without you. And it's an empowering and supportive thing when you give people the space and room to do exactly that. At first, they may be upset and call you selfish and tell you that you let them down, but the message you send to people when you put yourself first and give them the room to figure out their lives on their own is this: "I know you can handle this. I know that your life is your own and I'm not a requirement to you doing what you need to do in the same way that you're not a requirement to me doing what I need to do. I'm there for you but, in order to do that, I have to be there for myself first. I'm sure you'll understand."

When you resign as Manager of the Universe, you give yourself permission to focus on what you were put on this earth to do and you give other people the insight to see that they are powerful enough to do exactly what they need to do, whether you're involved or not. Even if it doesn't feel that way at the time, this is a very supportive, empowering, loving stance to take with anyone in your life.

Effective Way #2: Ask yourself the parent question and respond with immediate action.

I still struggle with feeling selfish and I definitely still struggle with putting myself first. In times when I know logically that I need to put myself first but emotionally worry about the aftermath of doing so, I use the parent question to get me back on track.

What is the parent question?

It's this:
If I had an adult child who was in my exact situation at the exact age I'm at right now, what advice would I give her?

It's amazing the answers you get when you ask yourself the parent question. All of a sudden, the resolve to make and keep yourself a priority becomes clear. If you're in a situation where you're a workaholic and have neglected your social, spiritual, fitness and family life in an effort to be the best at work, when you ask the parent question of "If my daughter was in a situation where she was a workaholic and sacrificing her health, her relationships, and her dreams for a job, what would I tell her to do?", all of a sudden, what YOU need to do becomes VERY clear.

Why? Because you can't guide your children down a path that you yourself aren't willing to model. When you ask yourself the parent question, you give yourself the answers you most need to hear. More than that, the struggle of feeling guilty for putting yourself first dissipates because you would never want your children to feel guilty for making themselves a priority in their own lives. You would tell them not to feel that way and you'd empower them to put themselves back on the priority list. If you're going to be a parent who gives that counsel, you have to be a person demonstrating what it means to live that advice.

Here's the other piece of this strategy: take immediate action with the parent advice you give. It's not enough to know what you 'should' do. You actually have to do it. So this effective way of getting over the idea of being selfish requires both thought and action.

Effective Way #3: Remind yourself constantly that you teach people how to treat you.

You are 100% responsible for the way you've allowed others to treat you. However you've been treated, you allowed it. You allowed the person or people to stay in your life. You've kept them as the priority you've maintained them at. You've given them unspoken permission to keep behaving the way they've been behaving. You've created the boundaries (or lack thereof) that you've created.

It's very easy to get caught up in the victim story of 'They did that to me' or 'Why do they treat me so badly?' Those might be accurate statements but they're not helpful. Until you can come to grips with the fact that you are constantly teaching people how to treat you, you won't get very far with reinventing your life.

Reinvention requires being real and calling things what they are. There is no reinvention without serious intention and intention is something that you can either create consciously or co-create subconsciously. Either way, you are the one setting and enforcing your boundaries, protecting your time, and devoting time to your highest priorities. If you aren't doing that in a way that allows you to create the life you want, it's not 'their' fault; it's yours. And it's really important to take full ownership of your role in how your life is working (or not working).

One of my favorite quotes from Tony Gaskins is this:

> *You teach people how to treat you by what you allow, what you stop, and what you reinforce.*

One of the best way to get over the idea of being selfish comes in reminding yourself that if you don't love you, if you don't make yourself a priority, if you don't set the goals that will create your best life and hold to achieving them, why should anyone else love you, make you a priority or honor the space you need to achieve the goals you've created? If you're not doing that for yourself, no one else will.

At the end of the day, don't take being called selfish personally. I know that's easier said than done but here's the thing: most of the time, the people who are calling you selfish are calling you selfish because you're not doing what they selfishly want you to do for them. You're not living according to **their** standards. They don't get to call the shots in your life and they're mad because they can't be selfish with your priorities. Put their criticism in proper perspective so you get where they're coming from and you know not to listen to that.

Always keep in mind that you MUST make yourself a priority because, at the end of the day, you will always be your longest commitment. On top of that, you can't give your ALL to anyone if you don't know how to give your ALL to yourself first. You might think you're giving your all to others but you can't give what you don't have.

See being selfish as a way of filling your tank and being ALL of who you are so you then have more to give to others. It truly is the only way to be a blessing to others. There is no helping others if you can't even help yourself. You can fake it but you aren't really doing it.

Keep that in mind…

CHAPTER REVIEW

At the end of each chapter, I want to provide you with an overview of what we discussed, specific strategies you can use, how to apply those strategies and what you can do to assess your results. Let's do our first chapter review…

The Concept

Get over the idea of being selfish. To reinvent your life, you're going to have to make yourself a top priority. You're going to have to devote MANY hours each week for MANY weeks to the reinvention process. You won't do that if you're not giving yourself permission to be selfish.

Selfishness creates WHOLENESS which then allows you to give fully to others later on. You can't give what you don't have.

The Strategies

There are 3 effective strategies you can use to get over the idea of being selfish:

1. <u>Resign as Manager of the Universe.</u> The Universe has everyone's back and you do not have to be the savior to all. Focus on being ALL that YOU need to create the life you want and, when you complete that reinvention process, you will have more than enough time to help others. In the meantime, while you're working on you, other people will have the opportunity and the space to see how powerfully they can solve their own problems. They'll learn that they don't need you to exist and that is a gift of a lesson that you're helping to teach.

2. <u>Ask yourself the parent question and take immediate action.</u> Whenever you feel like compromising your goals, dreams, standards and boundaries, ask yourself, "If my child was in this exact situation, what would I tell him or her to do?" and then do that.

3. <u>Remind yourself constantly that you teach people how to treat you.</u> What you allow is what will continue. Own that you've set up every relationship in your life to be the way it is. Examine what you're tolerating and change the game on what you're allowing from EVERYONE and EVERYTHING. When you do this, you will create more than enough space to reinvent your life. Yes, others will be pissed for a while (or a long time) but that's their problem, not yours.

The Application

1 **Post a reminder and read it often.**
For the next 14 days, I'd like you to write 'I resign as Manager of the Universe' on several post-it notes and put them in key places where you'll see those reminders on a daily basis. Make it your phone's screensaver if that helps. Any time you find yourself trying to be the Manager of the Universe, look at one of your post-it notes and say the

command out loud so you check yourself on trying to be everything to everyone.

2 **Use the parent question.**
Whenever you find yourself debating about whether to perform an activity or make a decision that puts you at the top of the priority list, ask yourself the parent question. Be sure to journal what your answer to the parent question is and go back to that every time you face a similar dilemma.

3 **For the next 7 days, observe how you get treated in all of your relationships.** This is not a time to set boundaries or to confront people about their behavior. I simply want you to notice the patterns of relationship that you've created, how people tend to treat you, and to what extent you've been tolerating that kind of behavior. Journal what you're noticing and, at the end of the week, review your journal notes and write down common threads, themes, and things you're noticing about what you're tolerating in relationships. Make a commitment to yourself that you'll start to shift any patterns that are not healthy for you.

Assessing Results

As you work on your reinvention process, I'd like you to set aside a minimum of 30 minutes at the end of each week to review what you've written in your journal, to make at least one new decision about how you're going to create more space and time for reinvention, and to draft a plan for the following week on what your daily schedule will look like (being sure to include time for reinvention and reflection).

At the end of two weeks, evaluate how well you've resigned as Manager of the Universe. Have you asked yourself the parent question and taken immediate action? Have you observed how you're being treated in your relationships? Are you now reflecting on ways you'd like to shift the patterns of interaction in those relationships?

Journal what you've accomplished in terms of results and find a way to celebrate your wins.

CHAPTER 3: MOVING FROM THE WHO TO THE WHY

Think like the person you want to become.
- **Unknown**

There was a time when I was a woman breadwinner coach. I coached women who were the financial breadwinners in their family… and I loved and hated it. Having been a breadwinner myself, I understood the challenges of being the breadwinner, the wife, the mother, working full time at work and working full time at home and never feeling like I could catch a break. Coaching this type of client came naturally because I'd lived that experience… only… something can come natural to you but not be meant for you… and that's what happened with coaching women breadwinners. I got to a point where I started dreading the calls. I knew that my time of coaching this particular population was quickly coming to an end… but there was fear.

I thought to myself:
Am I REALLY going to change target markets again?
Can I REALLY rebrand and revamp everything?
How many times do I need to shift markets before I stick with one?

The list of self-doubting questions and attacks went on for months. And then I finally hit my breaking point: this wasn't WHO I wanted to be in business and this wasn't leading me to my WHY for my business. The WHO and the WHY were insufficient to serve this population and when I got to that point, I knew I had to reinvent my business… and I did.

I now focus on creating online programs, tutorials and group coaching experiences for women who want to work on mindset. I help them fire their inner critics, find their inner badasses and finally build their businesses… and I love every single second of it! That is WHO I want to be in my business and my WHY for doing it is so strong that it gets me up in the morning and it excites me throughout the day.

I love to teach mindset. I'm a firm believer that if your mindset isn't right, nothing else works. And I get to that with every book I write, every talk I give, and every client that I'm blessed to work with.

So once you get over the idea of being selfish, the second step to reinvention is this:

Decide WHO you want to be.

If you could be EXACTLY who you want to be, what would that person be like?
What profession would you be in?
How would you see the world?
What kinds of relationships would you have?
What does your body look like?
How do you spend each day?
When you do wake up and go to sleep?
Where do you live geographically and how does it make you feel to live there?
What kind of impact do you have on the world?
What thoughts are you thinking on a regular basis?
What does a day in your life look like?
What do you believe about success, love, happiness and peace?
How would other people describe you?
How do you show up for others?
How do you show up for yourself?

The above are a small set of questions that you can ask and answer to get to the WHO of your reinvention. Here's the problem for most people: they fear answering the above questions because they doubt their ability to live into the answers. To explore and create your WHO, you have to be willing to dream big and go out on a limb. It takes practice to imagine yourself as a greater version of YOU that you've never been… especially when you've lived long enough to experience the worst of who you've been or to watch others try to become the best version of themselves… and fail time and time again.

So where do you start? How do you get over your fears, self-doubt, and anxiety about reinventing yourself to a point where you now become WHO you've always wanted to be?

In <u>Awaken the Giant Within</u>, Tony Robbins says the following:

Three decisions that you make every moment of your life control your destiny. These three decisions determine what you'll notice, how you'll feel, what you'll do, and ultimately what you will contribute and who you become. If you don't control these three decisions, you simply aren't in control of your life. When you do control them, you begin to sculpt your experience. The three decisions that control your destiny are: 1. Your decisions about what to focus on, 2. Your decisions about what things mean to you and 3. Your decisions about what to do to create the results you desire.

Notice that Tony hasn't even gotten to specific steps and actions to take and, yet, he's saying that those three things are literally what is deciding your future. Sit with that...

In order to decide WHO you want to be, there's mindset work that must be done first. Here's what that looks like:

In your journal, respond to the following:
1. Write out who've you've been, who you currently are and why you want to change who that is
2. Identify any flaws, limiting beliefs, negative life experiences, or current problems that you feel are getting in the way of you becoming the best version of yourself
3. Write down a list of decisions that you made in the past that got you to where you are today. These could be good or bad decisions.
4. What life choices have brought you to the present moment experience of your life?

Then, in the same journal, write out who you believe you're capable of becoming. Be as descriptive and specific as you can be. Respond to the following questions:
1. What standards would that version of you have for career, finances, relationships, health, social life, etc?

2. How does that you make decisions?
3. What kind of key life decisions would that version of you be making?
4. Can you close your eyes and see that version of you clearly?
5. What does that version of you think, believe and KNOW that the current version of you doesn't?

Write out the bio and description of that version of you as if you were casting a lead role for the movie.

Next, read both versions of the WHO out loud and ask yourself the following:

➢ What would have to happen in my life for me to get from the current version of me to the future state version of me?
➢ What leaps would I have to take?
➢ What decisions would I have to make?
➢ Who would I have to become to have all that I want?
➢ What are the specific steps I'd have to take to see myself in an entirely new way?
➢ What new skillsets, approaches, beliefs, and relationships would I have to acquire in order to become the best version of myself?
➢ Can I see myself doing that?
➢ Can I visualize what that version of me looks like in an every day situation?

Let me be very clear about this: this is a HARD exercise to do. It will take you a considerable amount of time, anywhere from hours to days and weeks to really think this through. Give yourself a week or two to complete this exercise. A lot of the delay in doing this comes from all of the negative self-talk you're going to grapple with as you complete the journal exercise. Your inner critic will rage. It's difficult to create a clear vision of WHO you want to become when your inner dialogue is mocking even the thought of you being any better than you are. Give yourself time. Give yourself room. Most importantly, give yourself grace to complete this assignment. Your soul knows the WHO you can become. You've simply got to clear the noise in your head and doubts in your heart to clearly articulate who that is.

Once you have the WHO written down, now you can get to the third step to reinventing your life:

Create the WHY you need to get there.

Why do you want to do whatever it takes to become the highest version of yourself?

The first response you give is your initial WHY and it'll be a good response but it's not the REAL reason you want to reinvent your life. You'll need to go seven levels deep and continue asking yourself WHY until you get to the response that produces a visceral, emotional, heart centered reaction in you. What you'll soon discover is that your initial WHY is far removed from your REAL WHY... and it's the REAL WHY that you'll want to refer to when the going gets tough or when you feel like giving up on your reinvention.

A powerful WHY does a number of things for you.

A powerful WHY:
- Helps you maintain your faith and determination to succeed
- Supports you in moments of temporary defeat and failure
- Keeps your focus on your long-term vision
- Enables you to stay the course and persist on your dreams
- Reminds you why you're working as hard as you're working
- Gives you the ability to ignore the critics and to keep going in the direction of your best life

The WHY is what keeps you going when everything in you wants to give up. Be sure that you've created a WHY that can be tested under extremely discouraging circumstances and major obstacles and still fuels you through them. That's the indication that you have a powerful WHY.

CHAPTER REVIEW

Let's review the major concepts in this chapter.

The Concept

Reinvention requires that you know WHO you want to become and WHY you want to become that version of yourself. Reinvention requires laser clarity. You must know WHO you have to become in order to have all that you want. That means knowing the details of the future version of yourself. You've got to know everything from what that version of you does for a living to how that version of you makes major life decisions. Getting clear on the WHO then allows you to get crystal clear on the WHY. In order to reinvent your life, you need a powerful WHY that will keep you going even in times where you want to give up. The WHY has to go seven levels deep and must be something that when you say it to yourself, it's a why-that-makes-you-cry and your WHY should do that every time you say it. If it doesn't, it's time to change the WHY. Your WHY is the secret weapon you use when you're under attack and feel like reinvention isn't something you'll be able to do.

The Strategies

Journal who you currently are and what you currently believe about yourself. Then journal who you would like to be and what that version of your thinks, feels and does differently in every day life. Journal your WHY and go seven levels deep. Every time you indicate your WHY, ask "Why?" again until you hit a WHY that's so powerful that it makes you want to cry.

The Application

1 **Write a story about your WHO.**
See yourself as a character in a movie and write the story of what your life, as the greatest version of yourself, looks like. After you've written the story, read it to yourself on a daily basis. You can read it every morning and every night. Get the essence of the WHO into your being with daily repetition.

2 **Write down your WHY and say it every morning.**
Before you start working on reinvention, pull out your WHY and say it out loud. When the going gets tough, pull out your WHY and say it several times until you can feel the power of it. The more time you spend reviewing and knowing you WHY, the less likely it will be that you allow temporary defeat to become permanent failure.

Assessing Results

Use both your WHO and your WHY to start making different decisions in your life. For example, you can ask yourself, "How would the future version of me make financial decisions? How would the future version of me show up in relationships? How would that version of me decide what to do next professionally?" And then make the decisions that your reinvented self would make and follow through in the exact fashion that your highest self would do.

CHAPTER 4: HOW TO CREATE A REINVENTION PLAN

Decide where you want to go and don't stop until you get there.
- Unknown

This chapter is dedicated to creating your reinvention plan. There are a few points of clarification that we need to get into first.

1 **Planning without execution is a total and complete waste of time.**
Creating a plan for reinvention is necessary but it is only an initial step. In this chapter, I'm going to give you a step-by-step breakdown of how to create a reinvention plan. This will take you anywhere from 3 to 10 hours to do. There's a lot to consider and there's a lot to organize and schedule so, yes, it's going to take a number of hours to develop a solid reinvention plan. But... that is only the beginning. You have to develop a doable plan with doable timelines and you have to be 100% committed to following through on EVERY step of the reinvention plan as indicated and as scheduled on your plan. If you're going to alter the order, priority or time of ANYTHING in your plan, it must be done at least a day in advance and cannot be shifted simply because you 'don't feel like' doing the things you need to do in order to reinvent your life. Stick-to-it-ive-ness is critical if you're going to see your plan through.

2 **You have to measure and document consistency on a daily basis.**
I talk about this in my Rebuild Yourself University. You've got to track your consistency. Whether that's using the tools I offer in Rebuild Yourself University, creating your own consistency tracker, or using an app like Habit Bull, you MUST be vigilant about making sure that by the end of each day, you know whether or not you did the things you need to do to experience your reinvention.

3

You have to review certain components of your reinvention plan on a daily basis. This is similar to the idea of writing down your yearly goals every day. In order to keep your reinvention as a top priority, you need to set aside 10 minutes a day to review your reinvention story, plan and weekly/monthly objectives. Here's the thing: if you don't know your daily, weekly and monthly reinvention targets, how are you going to know what to do to get there? You won't. This is a very strategic and vital component of creating your reinvention and it MUST be done on a daily basis. The best way to ensure that it gets done is to schedule 10 – 30 minutes on your calendar every day to review your reinvention plan.

Now… let's talk about the fourth step for reinventing your life:

Count the cost.

➢ What is it going to cost you to reinvent your life?
➢ How much time, money, energy, and focus will you need in order to reinvent yourself?
➢ What are you willing to give up, let go of, or sacrifice in order to fulfill your need for reinvention?
➢ What is your unwillingness to reinvent yourself costing you?
➢ How long have you been paying that price?

It's really important to count the cost of not reinventing your life as well as the cost to reinvent your life. Let's talk first about what NOT reinventing your life has been costing you. A lot of people turn down the idea of reinventing their lives due to all of the 'work' they believe it will take to do so. If they want to lose weight, they see the cost of giving up foods they love, having to make time to go to the gym, the social events and fancy dinners they'll have to turn down. Initially, something like a weight loss journey feels hefty in terms of the price you'll have to pay. But, let's look at the cost of staying at a weight that is unhealthy for you: increased doctor visits, medications, health complications, diabetes, losing your eyesight, losing a limb, going into a diabetic coma, heart disease, stroke, cancer, not being able to see your children grow up, not being able to walk your daughter down the aisle. These are long term serious costs that most people never consider because they don't want to believe that what they're doing today could lead to those horrible things. But they can and they will.

If you really want to create a reinvention that sticks, you have to say to yourself:

➢ What is the pain that I'm living with because I'm refusing to do the things I need to do in order to grow and reinvent myself?
➢ Why am I allowing myself to settle for mediocre?
➢ Why am I not taking FULL control of my life and creating the best ME I can?
➢ What is keeping me stuck and why am I allowing it to do that?

Get real with yourself and tell yourself the truth about why you're willing to sacrifice your life to stay in a place you don't really want to be.

The second cost is what reinvention will require of you. You have to look at the amount of time, energy, effort, and resources that your reinvention plan is going to require. Using the example of losing weight, there are a number of questions that will help you determine what the cost of investment will be for you.

➢ Do you have to sign up for a gym membership?
➢ How many hours a week will you be spending at the gym?
➢ Given your work hours and family commitments, what's going to be the best times for you to go to the gym?
➢ How can you make those non-negotiable appointments that you set and keep with yourself?

Be realistic. Err on the side of allocating more time, money and energy than less to your reinvention. Get very clear on what obligations you need to delegate and what commitments you need to renegotiate so you can create the time you need to reinvent your life. The only way you can see what needs to stay and what needs to go on your schedule is by adequately assessing the cost of investment for reinvention and even if you've never reinvented your life before, you can give yourself a ballpark estimate that will be pretty spot on when it comes to how much time, energy, and effort you'll need to give to your plan on a daily basis.

Step #5 to reinventing your life is this:

Forecast the timelines.

Now that we've counted the cost, it's time to assess what's reasonable in terms of reinvention. I'll use myself as an example. One of my reinvention goals is to get my body ready to step on stage for my first NPC Bikini competition. Now... I have A LOT of body fat to lose. This isn't something that's going to be a 12 week prep and then I can hit the stage and compete. Forecasting the timelines for this part of my reinvention means being reasonable about the amount of body fat I can lose each week, the amount of muscle I can gain each month, and the length of time it will take me to produce a physique that can win a competition. I also have to add in other variables that could change my timeline. For example, I know that I'm now in my forties and I want to have more children. I'm running out of time to do that so at the same time that I'm working to reinvent my body for competition, I'm also working to prepare my body for pregnancy and pregnancy (or pregnancies) will slow down the timeline to that first competition... and this is where most people get stuck. They say "Well, I can't really forecast getting back into shape because I never know what month I'm going to become pregnant and then I don't know when I'll have the baby or how long it will take me to stop breastfeeding so I'm not even going to attempt to forecast that goal because I have no control over picking the exact month and date when this and this is going to happen."

Let me be VERY clear: **those kinds of excuses are copouts.**

Here's how I'm looking at this timeline:

Pregnant or not, I want to have a super fit and healthy body. I have no idea when I'm going to get pregnant. I have no clue how long my next pregnancy will last but here's what I do know: in order to get my body fat down and my physique competition ready, I need about two solid years of consistent training and carb cycling. Two years... Notice I didn't say six months. It will take me AT LEAST one year to drop the body fat I need to drop and then AT LEAST another year to develop my muscularity to where it needs to be to compete. I'm not trying to shortcut the process because that is the fastest way to permanent failure for the goal, for my health and for my life.

So… two years is the minimum I need to prep for competition. I also know that, over these two years, I'm going to be trying to get pregnant. I have no clue which month will be "the" month. I don't need to know that. Here's what I do know: if I give myself double the amount of time to get competition ready (in this case, four years), I am factoring in a pregnancy or two in that timeframe. I might even forecast the timeline to be five years away just to be conservative with my forecast.

Do you see how that works?

It's critical that you forecast how long different parts of your reinvention will take while also including plenty of extra time to buffer in any 'life happening' situations that could delay you hitting that milestone. On the one hand, be conservative and, on the other hand, approach each day with absolute urgency and get shit done.

Here are some other examples of forecasting timelines for different parts of your reinvention:

> **Going back to college to get a degree-** if you have transfer credits and you want to be done in 2 years, add another year as buffer time (2 years added max)
> **Changing careers-** this depends on what has to be done in order to change your career. Factor in the time it takes to get additional certifications, skills, degrees, different jobs, and then add a year or two to that equation
> **Relocating to a different geographic location-** do the research on the cost of living, job opportunities, what it would take for you to find a job in that area or be granted a relocation with your current company. Determine how much money you'd have to save to relocate and how much you'll need to save every month (and for how long) in order to do that. Typically, if you're taking

daily massive action on a relocation and it doesn't involve a major emotional upheaval for children, spouses and others who may not be on board with the move, it should take you no longer than 1-2 years to both plan and do your relocation. If you have children in school and nobody wants to move or if you have a spouse who has a thriving career that he or she cannot leave, your relocation plan will take a lot longer to figure out and execute on but, even then, it shouldn't take any longer than five to seven years

Here's the thing I want you to understand from this step: Reinvention is NOT an overnight process. It really is a process that takes YEARS for almost any kind of lasting reinvention. We live in a world that's so addicted to showing a total complete life makeover in a thirty-minute episode. In this fast food world, people falsely believe that reinvention can happen quick. Now, your mindset can change in an instant. You can make new decisions at any moment and those new decisions can point you to an entirely different life but the full impact and result of those decisions will not be made manifest for YEARS. Get comfortable with that. Be committed to a long journey because, in most reinvention situations, that's what is required.

The sixth step to reinventing your life is this:

Develop a MAP (Massive Action Plan).

Your Massive Action Plan is your tactical, practical, strategic outline of every step of your reinvention process. It lays out everything from your personal mission statement to your reinvention story to your yearly, monthly, weekly and daily goals. It is an EXTENSIVE document that you must review every single day. The MAP will be what you use to follow through on the plan, to hold yourself accountable to the daily massive action of the plan, and to re-inspire yourself when you've hit a stuck point, a failure or you feel like this dream of reinvention is impossible. The plan needs to be something that you have in a binder, saved as a PDF on your phone, and, if you really want to get the plan into your very being, an audio recording that you record of yourself outlining the plan. That way, you can see it, read it and hear it on a daily basis so you become intimately connected to the nitty gritty details of the plan.

I've created a MAP workbook and outline for you that you can download at https://kassandravaughn.lpages.co/yourreinventionplan/. Please download it and use it as we go through the different components of your MAP.

Here's what goes into your MAP (Massive Action Plan):

1) **Your reinvention purpose**
    Your reinvention purpose states why you MUST reinvent your life. It's a two to three sentence personal mission statement that speaks to the WHY behind your reinvention.

2) **Your current state**
    Your current state is the description of where you currently are in your life. What's working? What's not working? How did you get here? Why are you off course? What is causing you pain? Why do those things need to change now? The current state tells the story of where your life is at this moment in time.

3) **Your future state**
    This is your reinvention story. It is the story you write (first in your own handwriting and then typed up as part of this reinvention plan) that details the WHO and the WHY of your reinvention. Who will you be by the end of this process? Why do you need to become that version of you? What will life look like when you get there? How will each day go? What will you feel, think and do that's different from the current you that exists? When you write your reinvention story, you write it as if it's already here now (i.e. in the present tense). It is your future YOU telling the story of that future as if it were already here now.

4) **Key results and outcomes expected**
    Identify the results and outcomes that will demonstrate to you that you've reinvented your life. These metrics will be different for different people. If you were to reinvent your life and show a complete stranger that you did, what evidence would that stranger need to see in your life to say 'Wow! You've done a complete

180!'? That will clue you into what your key results and outcomes should be.

5) **The Reinvention timeline and key milestones**
Create a timeline that shows dates, deadlines, and when key reinvention milestones need to be hit. Create a visual timeline that shows you what your future is going to look like and then work diligently to live into that future.

6) **Your reinvention priorities and sequencing**
Break down all of the things that you need to do to reinvent your life. Categorize them. Create a massive list of things that need to get done in each area of reinvention. Then take each list and break them down by priority and sequence. Priority is categorizing your to-do list from most to least important. Sequencing is indicating, once your priorities are straight, what specific steps need to happen first, second and third.

7) **Consistency Tracker**
A sample consistency tracker is supplied in the MAP workbook and outline that you can download in the FREE reinvention plan template found >>HERE<< or you can develop your own consistency tracker. You can also download an app like HabitBull to track your consistency over time.

8) **Resources and Support list**
Create a list of all of the resources and support you're going to need along your reinvention journey. This could be people, money, time, mentors, books, programs, courses, degrees, etc. Identify all of the resources you'll need for this journey.

9) **Accountability partner and cadence of accountability**
Identify who will be your accountability partner and the specific nature of that relationship. In other words, how often will you be in contact with your accountability partner? How often will your accountability partner check in with you? What happens if you don't do the things you say you're going to do? How will your accountability partner help you get back on track? The answers to these questions represent your selected cadence of accountability.

10) **Your reinvention calendar**

You have to schedule in EVERY bit of time that you need to work on your reinvention. Your schedule needs to reflect all the areas of your life: work, family time, brushing your teeth, cooking and eating. An accurate calendar will show you how much reinvention you have time for. It will also show you what things you need to delegate, get rid of or stop doing in order to create the time and space you need to work on your reinvention. You can see a sample calendar in the MAP workbook and outline found in the reinvention plan template found >>HERE<<.

11) **Review and assessment dates**

You should be reviewing your reinvention plan on a daily basis. On a weekly basis, you'll want to review your results, tweak your strategies and decide what to do differently next week.

12) **Celebration strategies**

What will you do to celebrate small and big wins? How will you celebrate the fact that you're even on the journey to reinventing your life? Create a system of reward and recognition BEFORE you start the reinvention process so you know exactly what to do when you follow through and make progress. Examples of celebration strategies can be found in the MAP workbook and outline found >>HERE<<.

13) **Things to remember when the going gets tough**

Pull together a list of 20-40 quotes that inspire, motivate and get you to take action. Put them in your MAP and keep the MAP in a binder close to you. In times of doubt and failure, open up to the section with those quotes and make yourself read EACH of the quotes out loud until you feel an emotional shift and want to take action.

14) **A list of role models who've done what you're going for**

You are not the first person to reinvent your life nor will you be the last. Include in your MAP a list of role models who've been where you've been, who've reinvented their lives, and are now happier, healthier and WHOLE for doing so. Every time you doubt your ability to proceed, pull out that list of role models, go find audio interviews or YouTube videos of them, watch them and remind yourself that "If that person can do it, so can I." It's a solid way to remind yourself that reinvention isn't rocket science. Anyone can do it.

CHAPTER REVIEW

Let's review the major concepts in this chapter.

The Concept

Your reinvention plan is critical AND it only works if you work it.
Developing your reinvention plan requires that you count the cost, forecast
the timelines and develop a MAP (Massive Action Plan). It's really
important that you be conservative on your timelines. With most big goals
or dreams, the time to fulfillment is typically twice as long as you originally
imagined. Rather than going into reinvention with a short-sighted
timeframe, double the timeframe in advance and work as hard as you can to
beat that deadline.

The Strategies

You can download the MAP workbook and outline (contained in the
Reinvention Plan template) >>HERE<< and it will guide you through the
process of developing your MAP. Prior to developing your MAP, you'll
need to spend a few hours in reflection. Use this time to assess the cost of
investment to reinvent your life. Also use the time to forecast how long
you think it will take to completely reinvent your life. Be conservative on
the timeline. Double the number of weeks, months or years you think it's
going to take with a goal of beating that deadline.

The Application

1 **Set realistic reinvention timelines.**
Your reinvention plan has to reflect the amount of time, effort and
energy you're willing to put into this plan for a LONG period of
time. Be sure that you get real with yourself about how much time
you're willing to invest, the boundaries that you need to set up to protect
your time and the length of time that it's going to take to complete your
reinvention process. Be accurate, realistic but also vigilantly focused on
achieving your reinvention in the least amount of time possible but in the
optimal amount of time needed to create a reinvention that can be
sustained over a lifetime.

2 **Create boundaries now.**

Decide now what your boundaries are going to be in terms of the time you're going to now devote to creating your best life. Have boundary conversations with those closest to you who will be impacted by the shift in your priorities. Let people know what the deal is, why that's important to you and why you're not going to budge on the time that you need for yourself. Have those boundary conversations now so there is no question from others about bending them later.

3 Review your reinvention plan DAILY.
This cannot be underscored enough. For this to become your primary focus, you've got to have your eyes on your reinvention plan every day... and you're not going to want to do that on days when you aren't delivering the necessary daily massive action to this plan. It's on those low performance days that you need to read your reinvention plan even MORE than on high energy, high performance days. When you're stuck, the fastest way to get unstuck is to remind yourself WHY you need to follow through on the commitment to reinvention that you made to yourself. Whatever it takes, force yourself to review your reinvention plan EVERY SINGLE DAY.

Assessing Results

Your consistency tracker and your calendar will be the methods by which you assess how closely you're sticking to your reinvention plan. The daily review of that reinvention plan will also tell you whether you're on or off track. Use all three to hold yourself accountable for daily massive action. Even better than that, get an accountability partner who can help hold you accountable on a daily basis. This will ramp up your level of commitment and consistency and will produce the results you've indicated in your reinvention plan.

CHAPTER 5: IT'S TIME TO SHOW UP DIFFERENTLY

You will never change anything that you are willing to tolerate.
- Myles Munroe

At this present moment, I'm going through a definite reinvention. I've created my reinvention plan. I read it daily and I'm on a mission to transform certain aspects of my life. One of those aspects is my health and fitness. It's probably one of my hardest areas to reinvent because it's an area that I've created a yo-yo reinvention pattern in. I've lost weight and gained it back. And I've done this at least four times in my lifetime.

Here's what's different about this current health reinvention: I'm taking the steps that I'm going to discuss in this chapter. Prior to starting my health reinvention, I created a new identity, an inevitable environment and I speak and act differently. Now, there's a lot of detail to this and I talk about my fitness journey on my YouTube channel at www.youtube.com/kassandravaughntv.

And here's the bottom line: reinvention only lasts if you become the version of you capable of sustaining it. Now, there's a lot to that statement. There is one version of you that's needed to create the reinvention but the version that created the reinvention is not the same person who'll be able to sustain it… and that's where most people go wrong.

When you begin your reinvention journey, you're hungry for change. You're eager, excited, determined, and probably frustrated enough to do whatever you have to do to change your life. This applies whether your reinvention is leaving a job you hate, a relationship that sucks, or losing the weight you've packed on. When you start the reinvention journey, your entire focus is "I NEED to change this NOW!"

Fast forward to completing the reinvention process. The sentiment "I NEED to change this NOW" won't motivate you to keep your changes.

You're no longer as hungry for the change because you've created it. You're no longer as motivated to do whatever it takes because you've done the internal work, produced the external results and your 'new' life isn't so new anymore. Welcome to your new normal… and that's where complacency sets in.

Now that you've made all the changes and you're reinvented, it's not new and exciting so an entirely different version of you has got to step up to the plate of your life and run the show if you're going to keep your reinvention.

How do you become that version of you?

You take steps 7 and 8 of the reinvention process and hold yourself accountable for doing them on a daily basis.

Step #7 to reinventing your life is this:

Set up an inevitable environment.

What does this mean? Eben Pagan originated the concept of inevitability thinking. Inevitability thinking is thinking and acting as if what you are pursuing is a done deal. It's whole heartedly believing that the outcome that you're going for is already done, is bound to happen and that your only focus needs to be on creating the conditions for which getting to the goal is inevitable.

Now… Step #7 goes beyond inevitability thinking. Step #7 to reinventing your life is the actual creation of an inevitable environment in which your reinvention is both created and sustained over time.

How do you do that?

Whether you're at the beginning of your reinvention process or have completed your reinvention, creating an inevitable environment requires that you ask and answer three important questions:

Question #1: How do I need to set up my life so that my reinvention (and maintaining of that reinvention) is inevitable?

Question #2: What are the non-negotiable parts of my day that will guarantee that I do the things I need to do to create and sustain my reinvention?

Question #3: What specific things do I need to eliminate from my life in order to guarantee that me slipping back into my old patterns will never happen again?

Let's work through an example. I'll use my NPC Bikini Prep journey with these three questions.

Question #1: How do I need to set up my life so that my reinvention (and maintaining of that reinvention) is inevitable?

My Response:
- ✓ I need to clear out the food pantry and fridge so that no sugary products or foods are found anywhere in my home.
- ✓ I need to meal prep once a week and ensure that I have EVERY meal I need to eat planned out and ready for use
- ✓ I need to meal prep at the same time on the same day every week. My meal prep time needs to be sacred and non-negotiable and have a weekly cadence that creates that ritual
- ✓ I need to lift weights and do cardio 6 days a week
- ✓ I need to take the necessary supplements on a daily basis
- ✓ I need to sleep a minimum of 6-7 hours a night
- ✓ I need to pre-plan and allow for cheat days, travel days and compensate for those by doing extra workouts
- ✓ I need to work out at the same time most days of the week so that this time block becomes sacred and non-negotiable
- ✓ Schedule my weigh-in, measurements, and progress pictures every four weeks

Given my response, there are a lot of details to set up. But once I make the above a system and I implement the system, after a few weeks, it'll become natural and, after a few months, it'll be easy. First it's going to be hard but, eventually, it's going to get easy. That's a key thing to remember when you're at the beginning of setting up your system for maintaining your reinvention.

Question #2: What are the non-negotiable parts of my day that will guarantee that I do the things I need to do to create and sustain my reinvention?

My Response:
- ✓ Weekly meal prep
- ✓ 6 day a week workouts at the same time for each day of the week (lifting and cardio)
- ✓ 6-7 hours of sleep a night
- ✓ Daily supplementation
- ✓ Filling out my consistency tracker every day

Question #1 helps you set up the system. Question #2 helps you identify what needs to get done on a daily basis to successfully live the system. There is some overlap between Questions 1 and 2 but it's important to identify what your daily non-negotiables are so you know whether or not you're holding to them.

Question #3: What specific things do I need to eliminate from my life in order to guarantee that me slipping back into my old patterns will never happen again?

My Response:
- ✓ Sugar
- ✓ Caffeine
- ✓ Wheat and gluten
- ✓ Going to bed later than 9 pm
- ✓ Eating out more than one time every two weeks
- ✓ Emotional eating
- ✓ Seeing results, getting overly confident and allowing a cheat meal to become a cheat day

By answering those three questions, I now know what system of eating and working out I need to set up. I also know what non-negotiable tasks need to be completed every day. I also know where my pitfalls are in advance so I can create coping mechanisms for them. If I want to take this even further, I can hire a bikini prep coach, watch videos from other competitors who've been where I've been and I can take notes on what strategies have worked for them. In this way, I can build a tribe of mentors and learn from their systems, apply it to my reinvention goal and then sustain it based on proven strategies for getting and keeping the reinvention.

Creating an inevitable environment means you structure your world, your life, and your day so you have no other choice but to follow through on you reinvention. While it's very simple, it's not necessarily easy. The most challenging piece of creating an inevitable environment comes from how uncomfortable the initial four to eight weeks of building and living in that environment will be.

Once you starting operating in an inevitable environment, your standards raise. You are now in new territory and not only will you have to adapt to the changes but so will everyone else around you. This is especially difficult if you've been tolerating far less than you deserve and have allowed your boundaries to be violated on a consistent basis. When you create an inevitable environment, you are now drawing a line in the sand and saying 'No more!' to far more than you know at the onset.

To create an inevitable environment, you have to become pretty strict with your habits, rituals and routines… and a lot of people won't understand why you've changed or why you can't continue to be who they want you to be. Add to this the fact that you're dealing with your own self doubt and fears about changing and you've got a situation where, on the one hand, you want to follow through and, on the other hand, you're afraid of what will happen when you do.

That's the tough part of creating an inevitable environment.

But here's the deal: either you want you reinvention or you're willing to keep the status quo. You can't have both and, each day, you are choosing one or the other, whether you realize it or not. Be sure that what you're choosing today is what you're good with living by tomorrow.

Step #8 to reinventing your life is this:

Speak and act differently.

I cannot say this enough: a different life requires a different you… and a different you starts with how you speak to yourself and about yourself. Your self-talk matters. It determines so much of your self-concept, your identity and your ability to persist and transform. Every action you take reflects your thoughts, feelings and inner dialogue. It doesn't matter what you 'want' to do. If you aren't internally congruent with being the person who can go out into the world and do that, you won't take daily, massive, inspired action. You might take tiny action. You might even take coerced action but you won't take fruitful action because fruitful action requires a powerful mindset.

To act differently, you have to show up differently. To show up differently, you have to think, speak and believe differently. The version of you that got you to the place of seeking reinvention thinks, feels, and behaves in a certain way. That version of you cannot get you to the place of reinvention that you want to be. A new life requires a new you.

How do you get there?

1. Drastically reduce the thoughts and speech that aren't serving you. Every time I complain, nag or gossip about other people, I can feel the downward spiral of that discussion. It's as if I'm allowing good things to seep away from me as I complain about what I don't like or talk about how other people are behaving. It's important to notice when your thoughts or speech are going in a direction that's moving you away from reinvention and either change the subject, stop the inner or outer dialogue or focus on what you're grateful for. That's not to say that you'll never complain, nag or gossip again. Your goal here is to drastically the reduce the amount of it that you do on a consistent basis.

2. Speak, move and take action like your future Self would.

How would your future Self handle today? What would your future Self be doing, feeling, thinking and pursuing today? Start with the next 24 hours and, for the next 24 hours, run your day from the perspective of the you that will exist after you reinvent your life. You'll be amazed by how differently you look at your day and how much more power you actually bring to your day because you've taken on the role of being the you you plan to become.

3. Create a post-it note or 3x5 notecard with this question and ask yourself this every 2 or 3 hours throughout the day: Does this support the life I am trying to create?

   This is a POWERFUL question because it forces you to assess and deal with the reality of what you are or are not giving to your reinvention. Every 2 or 3 hours, ask yourself the question "Does this support the life I am trying to create?" You'll immediately get your answer and if your answer is 'No', you need to follow up that question with "What do I need to do right now to fix that?" and then fix it.

The Concept

Set up an inevitable environment where failure is not an option. Speak and act differently so that your inner dialogue, your outer talk and your behavior are congruent with the YOU that you will become post-reinvention. Creating an inevitable environment is all about developing the system of daily rituals, habits, and behaviors that will facilitate your reinvention. Once you know what it will take to create an environment where you cannot fail, it's up to you to actually create and live in that environment. Speaking and acting differently requires that you micromanage your self-talk, pay close attention to what you're saying to others and deliver speech and behavior that's in alignment with who you want to become.

The Strategies

Determine what an inevitable environment looks like for you. Eliminate anything that could jeopardize that inevitable environment. Find mentors who have proven systems for creating the kind of reinvention you're trying to create and implement their systems into your daily approach to life. Speak and act from the place of already being the version of you that you'll be once your reinvention process is complete. Make decisions from that place. Take action from that place. Think, feel and operate from that place.

The Application

1 **Use the information in this chapter to create your inevitable environment today.**
It will take you anywhere from 1 to 3 hours to create the systems you'll need. It may take you a few more hours to research and/or pinpoint mentors who have proven systems. Overall, you'll probably spend 4-8 hours creating the systems, practices, and routines that will represent your inevitable environment. Do not do anything else before you do this. Set up and implement your inevitable environment in the next 48 hours.

2 **Go on a complaining fast for the next 48 hours.**
For the next 48 hours, cut out ALL complaining. Yes, it will be hard. Yes, this includes mental, inner complaining. Yes, you'll have to micromanage your thoughts. Do it and see how much space you free up to think, feel and behave like the reinvented version of you you plan to become.

Assessing Results

Once you've created your inevitable environment, put the different daily tasks or actions in your consistency tracker and track your completion of those things for the next 2 weeks. After 2 weeks, evaluate how consistent you've been on creating your inevitable environment. Tweak your approach so that you can get to 100% consistency within the next 60 days.

CHAPTER 6: HOW TO BELIEVE IN YOURSELF WHEN NO ONE ELSE DOES

Fairy tales are more than true: not because they tell us that dragons exist, but because they tell us that dragons can be beaten.
- Neil Gaiman

I LOVE super hero movies. Batman, Incredible Hulk, Black Panther, Thor, Ironman, The Bionic Woman, Wonder Woman, you name it, I love it!

Why?

Because we all live the hero journey and superhero movies remind me that it's possible for any person to go from mortal to immortal, from average to extraordinary, from mediocre to exceptional because everything they need to activate the superhero is within them. It's lying dormant and simply requires the commitment, consistency and intensity necessary to bring that side of you to the forefront.

I also love superhero movies because there are moments in those stories where the superhero has no support. Families criticize. Friends betray. Even strangers can't be trusted. For the superhero, there are parts of the journey that he or she must go through alone... and it's so true to life.

It's also true that the superhero, at some point in the movie, experiences a fall. The hero is incredible for a while and then here comes this unforeseen villain or obstacle that completely throws the superhero for a loop... and that person has to find the strength and faith within to transcend the failure and become even more powerful than she was before... and here's the clincher: that superhero has to find it on his own. It can't be given to the superhero by someone else.

And that's the power of believing in yourself when no one else does. If you are serious about reinventing your life, you have to know that many people will doubt you. They've never seen you create and sustain a reinvention. Some of them enjoy the fact that you aren't your most powerful self. Others are so afraid of who you'll become post-reinvention that they're doing their best to convince you to not want or go for more.

So this chapter is designed to teach you how to believe in yourself when no one else does so you stay the course on your reinvention and get to where you truly want to be.

The ninth step to reinventing your life is this:

Keep your commitments to you.

You have to draw a hard line on this. Even one missed commitment to yourself creates a huge ding to your self-esteem, self-worth and faith in your ability to reinvent your life. If you make a promise to you, you MUST keep it at all costs. There can be no ifs, ands or buts about this. And make no mistake: this is the key decider of whether your reinvention lasts… which is why it's important to only make the commitments to yourself that you know you can keep.

For example, if you want to change careers and a key piece of that reinvention is going back to school, you need to make the commitment to apply for a program by a certain date AND keep that commitment no matter what. You then need to make the commitment, once accepted, to start by a certain date, and keep that commitment NO MATTER WHAT.

This is a 0/100 strategy. Every single time you break a commitment you make to yourself, it crushes your self-esteem. You literally push yourself in the direction of not believing in yourself and then you become super susceptible to the opinions, skepticism and judgment of others. You've got to get to the point where you take a hard line and say "I keep the commitments I make to myself BEFORE I make any commitments to anyone else and I have no problem saying No to other people or renegotiating a commitment I make to someone else if it conflicts with me being able to keep the commitments I make to myself. Period. End of story. That's how this works."

And you don't have to start with big commitments to yourself. If you're on a fitness journey, start by making a commitment that you're going to drink a certain number of ounces of water a day. Create the habit in <u>Habit Bull</u>. Track it for 66 days and don't make any other commitments until you've kept that one commitment for 66 days. Keeping that one commitment, as minor as it might seem in the grand scheme of your reinvention plan, will go a long way in building your self-confidence, faith and feeling of certainty that you can and will reinvent your life.

Once you start making and keeping little commitments to yourself, gradually move into making bigger commitments to yourself. Over time, you'll find that you'll take a hard line on your commitments and you'll create healthy boundaries and so No to others with ease. This is a process that can take some time. It's not an overnight shift. Give yourself at least three months to create a habit of keeping your commitments to you.

The tenth step to reinventing your life is this:

Choose to believe in yourself when no one else does.

Here's the thing: this is a choice EVERY single time. No one can teach you how to believe in yourself if you're not willing to trust yourself and faithfully believe in your ability to reinvent your life. You should never be deciding whether or not you believe in you based on whether or not other people believe in you. That's the fastest way to give other people control over your life and, in doing so, erase your sense of self-worth and personal power. Use other people's lack of faith in you to firm up your belief in yourself.

Distance yourself from people who only want to talk to you about how much you've failed or how little you've accomplished. Those people are not helping you evolve. They're invested in keeping you the same. In fact, they probably thrive from knocking you down. That's not the tribe of people you want to spend your time with. Get clear about who's on your team and who's not and remember that when you hit your reinvention and, all of a sudden, the people who were bashing you now want to be your BFF. Don't be fooled by fair weather friends or family.

Here's the thing: if you weren't with me when I had nothing, you don't get to be with me when I have everything. That's called having high standards... and the highest standard you could hold is the standard that tells everyone in your life "Don't worry about me. I don't need you to believe in me. I've got my own back." In this way, you free the right people to support you without the weight of obligation and you free the wrong people to exit your life because their lack of support will not be tolerated by your clear sense of self-worth.

We're now at the end of the book and there are a few things I need you to know:

1. *Reinvention is a choice and it's a choice you'll have to make every single day of your life.* This is not a one-and-done situation. If your reinvention is going to last a lifetime, you have to continually choose reinvention, choose evolution, and choose to be the person who is capable of holding onto that.

2. *Not everybody is going to be on board with you reinventing your life.* You're going to get a lot of flack and a lot of backlash from unexpected places and people. You're going to see how much fear and jealousy run some people's lives by the way they treat you when you have the 'nerve' to want more for your life and actually go out there and get it. Do not be dismayed by the opposition that shows up. It's all a spiritual classroom that you came to master. Embrace it for the growth opportunity that it is but also be SUPER clear about who's on your team... and who's not.

3. *You're going to want to give up a lot and especially if you have a hard time visualizing what your reinvented Self looks like.* In moments when you don't believe that your reinvention is possible and you question whether this is a reinvention you can create and sustain, compartmentalize the doubt and focus completely on the present moment actions you need to take. This is where having the reinvention plan printed out and in a binder becomes so important. When in doubt, go read the reinvention

plan. Ask yourself, "What next step am I supposed to be taking right now?" and go do that step. Forget about five years from now. You can't see that yet. Simply go back to the plan and work the plan.

4. ***Reinvention requires a lot of hard work.*** This is not going to be easy. You're going to have to fight for every ounce of evolution you create. Do not assume that this is a law-of-attraction-create-a-vision-board-go-to-bed-and-wake-up-an-entirely-different-person approach. Yes, your choice to go on the reinvention journey will automatically put you in a different mindset. Yes, every step you take on your reinvention journey will transform you. But, no, this is not going to be easy and you're going to have to fight to get there. Do not be discouraged by this idea. Earning the life you want is far better than someone else dictating the life they believe you can have. Be willing to do whatever you have to do to own your life, EVERY bit of it.

5. ***Focus on you and leave everyone else out of the equation.*** Don't try to figure everyone else out while you're working on you. You simply don't have enough energy or time to do that. Do not try to make major life decisions about relationships while you're working on you. Become the best version of you FIRST and then your Inner Knowing will tell you exactly what to do about every relationship in your life second. Keep this in mind: you will never make a powerful relationship decision from a place of being disempowered. You need to be your most powerful self to make your most powerful decisions. Can you make those decisions disempowered due to necessity? Yes, you can. A woman who's in a physically abusive relationship can't wait until she becomes powerful enough to leave it. Her life is on the line. However, if you're not in a dire, life or death situation, postpone trying to figure out major areas of your life all at the same time, focus on you, do the work of reinventing you and, once you do, everything that needs to leave your life, come into your life, or change in your life will become crystal clear and you will make all of the right decisions for you. Build yourself up first and then you'll know how to restructure everything else in your life.

At the end of the day, reinvention is what we were born for. Nature reflects this. Our physical bodies are constantly demonstrating this principle. Our cells regenerate all the time. Every bit of our physical and emotional body is transforming without us even knowing it. Reinvention is what we do. Decide today that you're ready to reinvent your life and create the life that you want. More importantly, decide then act.

Decisions without actions are wishes.
Decisions followed by immediate action are destiny.

WOULD YOU LIKE TO KNOW MORE?

Seeing individuals step into their full power is one of my life purposes. I fulfill that mission in a number of ways and I invite you to join me on the journey.

Rebuild Yourself
Are you ready to rebuild your life? Are you tired of settling for less than you deserve? Do you recognize that it's time to make some major shifts in your beliefs, your intentions and the direction you're taking your life? Check out Rebuild Yourself University, a 2-year online program, at www.kassandravaughn.com.

She Runs The Show
If you're a woman entrepreneur, an aspiring entrepreneur, or have any female friends who are thinking about entrepreneurship, invite them to join the movement and visit my blog at http://www.sherunstheshow.com. I host monthly teleseminars, webinars, and offer online programs that help women take their businesses to the next level. I also host an iTunes podcast for She Runs the Show. You can find the latest episode at: http://tinyurl.com/sherunstheshowpodcast.

Looking for a speaker?
I love to facilitate workshops, lectures, and conference talks on the topics of focus, resiliency, grit, personal power, and self-worth. If you'd like to discuss my speaking at your event or creating a corporate workshop for your company, please contact me at info@kassandravaughn.com.

Check out my other books
I love to write about overcoming fear and developing focus. Feel free to check out my other books at www.overcomingfearbooks.com.

If you have any questions, comments, or feedback, please email me at
info@kassandravaughn.com.
I'd love to hear from you!

DID YOU LIKE THIS BOOK?

If you liked the book, please recommend the book to friends, family, and any person you know who needs to read this. Also, please leave a review on Amazon and let me know how you felt about the book and what the book was able to help you accomplish. I'm always checking the reviews.

I'd love to respond to you personally. After you've left your Amazon review, please email me at info@kassandravaughn.com to let me know. Thanks in advance!

Kassandra Vaughn

ABOUT THE AUTHOR

Kassandra Vaughn is the CEO of SK Media LLC, an education and multi-media training firm that provides personal development and inner leadership training to individuals and organizations around the world. Author of over 10 books, Kassandra's mission is simple: to uplift and change people's minds about the greatness of their lives. From her work as a mentor and coach to her current work helping individuals develop redefine self-worth, increase self-belief and develop inner leadership skills, Kassandra's mission is to help people transform their limiting beliefs, rewrite their life stories and activate the leader within.

Made in the USA
Monee, IL
12 February 2020